MW01526244

SHOULD 360-DEGREE FEEDBACK BE USED ONLY FOR DEVELOPMENTAL PURPOSES?

SHOULD 360-DEGREE FEEDBACK BE USED ONLY FOR DEVELOPMENTAL PURPOSES?

David W. Bracken
Maxine A. Dalton
Robert A. Jako
Cynthia D. McCauley
Victoria A. Pollman

with Preface by
George P. Hollenbeck

Center for Creative Leadership
Greensboro, North Carolina

The Center for Creative Leadership is an international, nonprofit educational institution founded in 1970 to advance the understanding, practice, and development of leadership for the benefit of society worldwide. As a part of this mission, it publishes books and reports that aim to contribute to a general process of inquiry and understanding in which ideas related to leadership are raised, exchanged, and evaluated. The ideas presented in its publications are those of the author or authors.

The Center thanks you for supporting its work through the purchase of this volume. If you have comments, suggestions, or questions about any CCL Press publication, please contact the Director of Publications at the address given below.

Center for Creative Leadership
Post Office Box 26300
Greensboro, North Carolina 27438-6300
336-288-7210 • ww.ccl.org

Center for
Creative
Leadership
NORTH AMERICA EUROPE ASIA
www.ccl.org

©1997 Center for Creative Leadership

All rights reserved. No part of this publication may be reproduced, stored in a retrieval system, or transmitted, in any form or by any means, electronic, mechanical, photocopying, recording, or otherwise, without the prior written permission of the publisher.

CCL No. 335

Library of Congress Cataloging-in-Publication Data

Should 360-degree feedback be used only for developmental purposes? / David Bracken
   . . . [et al.].
         p.   cm.
      Includes bibliographical references.
      ISBN 1-882197-31-3 [ISBN-13: 1-882197-31-6]
      1. 360-degree feedback (Rating of employees). I. Bracken, David. II. Center for
   Creative Leadership.
   HF5549.5.R3F576 1997
   658.3'125—dc21   97-28278
                                                                                   CIP

Table of Contents

Foreword

There is an important discussion taking place today that seems to renew itself whenever people concerned with individual and organizational development get together. It revolves around the question, should 360-degree feedback be used only for development or should it also be used for administrative purposes such as deciding who gets raises and promotions?

Its importance notwithstanding, this discussion is detailed, complex, and not infrequently confusing. Which is why a debate on the topic held at the 1996 meeting of the Society for Industrial and Organizational Psychology (SIOP) so impressed those of us from the Center for Creative Leadership (CCL) who attended it. The four presenters—David Bracken, Maxine Dalton, Robert Jako, and Victoria Pollman—aided by a skillful moderator—George Hollenbeck—were able to clearly and efficiently lay out the essential issues. It was soon decided that CCL, via its report series, would make their presentations available to a wider audience: thus, the preface and four papers you will find here.

At the same time, in order to emphasize the ongoing nature of this discussion and to represent some of the reactions of the audience of professionals who viewed the debate, it was also decided that the report should add a voice to those mentioned above: thus, the fifth paper by Cynthia McCauley.

I am confident that readers will find these papers as stimulating and informative as I have. The professional stature of the author comes through clearly in each piece. This report is not, of course, a final answer to the question of how to use 360-degree feedback. I believe, though, that ultimately this discussion may prove most valuable not because it yields one right answer (although many people naturally long for one) but because it helps us better understand the potential of 360-degree feedback, no matter how we choose to use it.

Walter W. Tornow
Vice President, Research and Publication
Center for Creative Leadership
September 15, 1997

Preface
George P. Hollenbeck

In the fall of 1995 I was one of the lucky ones David Bracken called when he was seeking participants for a program at the 1996 annual meeting of the Society for Industrial and Organizational Psychology (SIOP) in San Diego. David was putting together a program that would deal with the tension between two main uses of 360-degree feedback: using it as a development tool for "assessed" managers and executives versus using it for administrative decision-making—serious things such as pay, promotion, and who goes on the fast track. David's thought was that a debate at SIOP would be lively and informative and would get the issues out on the table. He sensed that the time was ripe.

How right he was: 360-degree feedback has become a major tool of modern organization management. We heard one colleague describe it as the greatest innovation in the field of I/O psychology in twenty-five years. If I/O psychology ever had a claim to 360-degree feedback, the technique has long since been commandeered by a wide range of practitioners. Who could begin to guess how many managers will be subjected to 360-degree feedback next year! Like it or not, 360-degree feedback has become an accepted fact in organizations today, and its use is still growing.

A recent experience illustrates this point: A month ago I attended a "training" session for executive coaches who would be providing 360-degree feedback to all of the managers and executives in a company with more than 50,000 employees. Sitting at my left around a conference table of twenty or so was the vendor who provided the statistical services for this company, as well as for many others. "Robert," I asked, "has the fad peaked?" "Not on your life," he replied with a smile on his face. "I am adding staff every month."

If there is anyone left who needs to be reminded, 360-degree feedback is the process of "feeding back" to a person (usually a manager or executive) how others see him or her. The "others" are typically bosses, peers, and direct reports; sometimes they are others outside the immediate organization (for instance, internal or external customers). To quote from a BellSouth personal development guide produced in 1991: "You stand at the center of a circle of feedback sources. These sources are the people who know you best. They are the people whose opinions you trust; at work, at home, and in the community." Although this description perhaps unduly emphasizes opinions you can trust, the various points (0 degrees, 90, 180, and so on) of this feedback "circle" is where the term *360 degrees* came from. Although you will see in these papers a variety of favorite terms, such as *upward feedback, multisource feedback* (MSF), *multi-rater feedback* (MRF)—and these may satisfy the behavioral scientists' need for precision—in fact, these terms have lost the battle of the popular press to the fetching ring of *360-degree feedback*. And, worse yet for the purists, 360-degree feedback is widely used to describe feedback from whatever source, whether from the complete circle or not.

It is worth taking a few words to reflect on why 360-degree feedback has become so widely accepted now rather than twenty or forty years ago. After all, the basic survey methodology it uses has been in place since the 1950s, and equally early in our history the notion of using survey data to improve individual management performance was being explored. Maloney and Hinrichs (*Personnel*, July/August 1959; "A New Tool for Supervisory Self-development Personnel") described a "new" tool for developing managers at Esso Research and Engineering Company that looks teasingly close to a current 360-degree instrument. It asks employees to rate their supervisor on such items as "Gives you room for individual initiative," "Lets you know when he has criticisms of your work," "Lets you make the decisions you should make"—all items that might appear on a form from the 1990s. What happened? Why didn't 360 thrive in the 1950s? Primarily, I would argue, because "the boss was king" in those years, and "rate your manager" programs such as the one developed at Esso never took off. Several other pieces needed to be in place.

One of those pieces was the T-group movement of the late 1960s and early 1970s. Although the unrestrained pursuit of "open communication" and "letting it all hang out" turned out to be too volatile for most organizations, the T-group thrust changed the climate. It popularized and made legitimate the theme that feedback is an important ingredient of change and a key element of system performance.

On a parallel track to T-groups, the growing body of research on performance appraisal indicated that subjective ratings by the boss left a great deal to be desired. As the hopes for traditional, trait-based performance appraisal faded, most companies shifted to some form of management by objectives (MBO)—the forerunner of what has today come to dominate under the term *performance management*. With objectives and measurement standards on the table, it was only a small step until measurement standards included not only *what* results were achieved but also *how* they were achieved.

A whole series of forces drove the change from what a manager gets done (results) to how he or she achieves those results (how he behaves, what he says, how he treats people, and so on). Some of these forces were: (1) a changing employee population, with better educated baby boomers expecting to be treated differently; (2) social legislation—EEOC, OSHA, EPA, Foreign Corrupt Practices Act—placing constraints on how a company and its managers act; and (3) the changing nature of work; increasingly, the work that needed to get done was not manufacturing but technology, ideas, and information.

Another piece was the quality movement. Caught with their proverbial pants down, as foreign competition began making better products cheaper, companies in the U.S. began all-out efforts to catch up. Suddenly, everyone was a customer—not just those who buy our products but other departments, suppliers, even our employees. And surveys could provide the data to answer the question, "How am I doing?"

U.S. companies' drive to compete brought forth yet another piece, namely newer organizational forms such as teams, flatter organizations, and real decentralization in boundaryless organizations. With spans of control or influence that might cover seventy-five employees or customers scattered throughout the globe, traditional "supervision" was no longer possible. With new pressures to find out what your managers were doing, new ways were needed to find out what was going on.

One more piece and I rest my case. A result, or a part of, the "new organization" is the much-described "new employment contract" that shifts the burden of keeping up onto the shoulders of the employee: Companies don't develop managers anymore; managers develop themselves. Companies no longer promise employment; they promise employability. And if I as a manager am responsible for driving my own development, then I need data (feedback) to plan my course. Given the fact that my boss has, since time began, been reluctant or unable to provide very good data, what better tool than 360-degree feedback?

No doubt the reader can fill in the whole of my analysis with additional pieces. The fact is that eventually, as the most admired executive in the U.S., GE's hard-nosed Jack Welch, has been heard to say, GE executives can get fired for *what they do* as well as *what gets done*; results are no longer enough.

What better tool than 360-degree feedback to inform us about what an executive does?

It is not surprising that, given its multiple origins, there is disagreement over how 360-degree feedback should be used today. The presenters, skillfully chosen by Bracken, effectively represent the major positions in the dispute. Maxine Dalton of the Center for Creative Leadership is, I suspect, a natural-born defender of the development side; her passion for development comes through in her paper. Vicki Pollman has "seen it all" at places such as Texaco, and that perspective is revealed in her presentation. David Bracken, with his experience as co-founder of the Upward Feedback Forum, a consortium of more than twenty companies sharing issues on 360-degree feedback, reflects the desire of consulting clients to use data to evaluate. Robert Jako has hands-on experience in the nation's largest medical-delivery organization, Kaiser Permanente.

As the moderator, I saw my mission as making sure that the positions were clearly delineated so that the audience could more easily follow the spoken debate. To this end, I asked each of our presenters to make bald statements, which they did. In preparing their remarks for printed publication they have naturally modified some of these remarks. It is only fair for me to share the blame for any overstatements that might remain.

WHEN THE PURPOSE OF USING MULTI-RATER FEEDBACK IS BEHAVIOR CHANGE

Maxine A. Dalton

I will argue here that instrumented multi-rater feedback (MRF) is best used for developmental purposes and, therefore, should be a confidential and private process. MRF data should not be used for administrative, evaluative, or decision-making purposes.

In my experience the reason most often given for the use of instrumented MRF in an organization is to initiate behavior change in the person who is to receive the feedback. Whether the feedback is being given to problem performers or high-potentials, it is presented to the individual as baseline information from a variety of perspectives—an opportunity to see ourselves as others see us. The rationale behind this activity is that a person cannot become more effective, improve, or design a plan of development without first having baseline data about his or her current level of performance against some standard.

To satisfy this objective—a change in behavior as a response to MRF information—the data must be of high quality and the person must accept the data.

In this essay I will first comment on these two points: conditions that increase the likelihood that a feedback report will be based on reliable, veridical data; and the conditions that facilitate an individual "being able to hear" disconfirming information about him- or herself.

The Quality of the Data

I will approach this topic with both anecdotal and quantitative data. As I have been working with MRF surveys for a number of years, I have gathered many stories about multi-rater interventions. Undoubtedly, my belief system has created a filter for my retention and recall. Nonetheless, I will first describe the case, as I have seen it play out, and then will address the quantitative support for my argument.

Typically, when peers and subordinates are asked to rate their colleague and boss, respectively, they express concern about how these ratings will be used and if the individual will know "what I said." If the peers and subordinates like the individual they are being asked to rate, they are concerned about doing or saying anything that might hurt him or her. It might, therefore, be expected that either positive halo or restriction of range will mute the message. If raters dislike the individual they are being asked to rate, they may fear retribution or decide that this is a good chance to get even. Again, the data may reflect restriction of range or a negative halo.

If raters think the individual has a "good" boss, they may decide to trust him or her with the "truth." If they think the individual has a "bad" boss, they may be less willing to be forthcoming and candid. Typically, to address the issue of retribution and accountability and increase the likelihood that raters will provide candid feedback, they are guaranteed anonymity.

As to the use of the data, when raters are assured that the data will be used for confidential purposes only, they are relieved and much more willing to be candid and use the entire range of the scale.

These experiences are supported in the literature. Farh, Cannella, and Bedeian (1991) reported that when peers rated colleagues for evaluative rather than for developmental (confidential) purposes, the ratings showed greater halo and were more lenient, less differentiating, less reliable, and less valid. They concluded that "other things being equal, the more severe the perceived consequences of a negative rating, the greater incentive for the rating to be lenient." Hazucha, Szymanski, and Birkeland (1992) reported that boss and self scores on a multi-rater survey were higher under conditions of open feedback than under conditions of confidential feedback. London and Smither (1996) reported that forty percent of the raters interviewed after giving feedback under confidential conditions said they would change their ratings if the situation changed to an appraisal condition.

Accepting the Data

It is likely that a significant proportion of individuals receiving feedback from a multi-rater instrument will learn that they rate themselves higher than others do. Those who have studied self/other agreement on MRF instruments have reported that approximately one-third of the self-raters are likely to describe themselves in a more favorable light than their subordinates (see, for instance, Fleenor, McCauley, & Brutus, 1996).

Depending on the skills, traits, and attributes being rated, an individual may be receiving information about a personal quality that is core to the image of self, one's persona in the world. At best, this is an unsettling experience. At worst, it is devastating.

But it is not surprising. The typical workplace is not feedback-rich. Employees can work for years without a performance appraisal. Individuals can receive promotions and regular raises right up until the day they are dismissed for behaviors that they never even knew were considered a problem. And so it is not hard to understand that self-ratings tend to be higher than observer ratings for many people or that individuals can be "knocked out of their socks" by an MRF experience.

Therefore, to be able to take in instrumented feedback information, process it, evaluate it, integrate it, and make plans to learn new skills because of it, an individual must feel safe. In the struggle to reorganize self-image in response to the evaluations of others, a person must believe that the process does not make him or her unreasonably vulnerable. He or she must feel a high degree of psychological safety.

Traditionally, a cornerstone of psychological safety has been the convention of confidentiality. All of the tenets of counseling and therapy in the Western world are based on this convention, the belief that individuals are most likely to change if they can enter the process of self-discovery with a qualified person in a confidential setting—where the information disclosed and discussed will not be used against the individual who has undertaken a personal journey of self-discovery. This convention has even been codified for psychotherapists in most states, except in cases of child abuse or threats of murder or suicide.

Of course, MRF in organizations is not therapy, but it is about facilitating behavioral change. When MRF is collected and used for evaluative purposes—for making decisions about performance, promotion, salary increase—within a semipublic forum, then the process is no longer safe. The individual is highly vulnerable and, it is this writer's argument, much more likely to argue with, deny, reject the data, and fail to change.

In a breakthrough study on performance-appraisal processes conducted at GE in 1965, Meyer, Kaye, and French found just this outcome. Individuals who received negative evaluations from their boss that were tied to salary decisions rejected the data, and those who received the greatest number of criticisms during the appraisal process actually registered a decrement in performance. Meyer and colleagues recommended that coaching about performance for the purpose of improving performance be separated from salary decisions and that this coaching be a day-to-day and not a once-a-year activity.

Not only does the evaluative climate increase the likelihood that the data will be rejected (and therefore reduce the likelihood of behavior change), this climate also increases the stress associated with the feedback event.

To receive discrepant feedback is stressful. Individuals may perceive the stressful event as challenging, threatening, or harmful (Folkman & Lazarus, 1985). If the individual defines the feedback event as challenging, he or she may see this as an opportunity to use the feedback as a catalyst for change. If the individual determines that the stressful event is threatening or harmful—something that will block a promotion or a salary increase—he or she is more likely to use a different set of coping strategies, including denial, a damaging venting of emotions, or behavioral and mental disengagement (Carver, Scheier, & Weintraub, 1989). Even worse, if the boss who has access to the multisource feedback is not a skilled coach, or is himself or herself a punitive person, the feedback event may escalate into a truly unpleasant and unhelpful activity.

The Motivation to Make the Process Public and Evaluative

There are a number of motives for making the multisource feedback process public and evaluative. Some are benign, some less so. Some are laudatory but naive to issues of power and retribution.

A frequently cited reason for making feedback evaluative and public is the following: "How can we make the person change if we don't know what the feedback says?" Such a question represents the expressed manifestation of a personal theory of behavior change: Individuals change through punishment, retribution, and fear—the stick. This is an example of the construct of coercive power (Raven & Kruglanski, 1970) and produces a change in behavior that can only be maintained by monitoring, surveillance, and watchfulness. As Meyer and colleagues (1965) demonstrated, the outcome may also be a demoralizing psychological reaction in which performance actually declines.

A second reason for wanting to make multisource feedback public and evaluative is to provide greater rater input into the process of appraisal. The argument is a liberal one, based on a vision of egalitarian and collaborative organizational structures. It is an appealing argument: "Why should the boss be the only one to have a say in the appraisal process?" Despite its appeal, it is naive about issues of power and retribution. A rater might be told that his or her ratings of the boss will be anonymous, but the average score of five 1s is still 1; it does not seem too big a leap to surmise that the individual who receives such a score is the individual least likely to have the interpersonal skill to cope with the knowledge that all of the raters described him or her in such a fashion.

Individuals in organizations need feedback and they need it from multiple sources. They cannot be expected to change their behavior without the 360-degree perspective that tells them that their message is not being received as intended. The goal of an instrumented program of multisource feedback should be to move toward the day when instrumentation is no longer necessary, when appraisal is not an annual event, when enlightened individuals are able to let one another know "in the moment" about the impact of a set of behaviors on the work task so that recalibration can begin immediately. The core of this argument about the use of multisource feedback is how do we get there. It is my argument that instrumented multisource feedback is a tool in service to this goal, but that it is a tool that must not be used as a blunt instrument.

Rather, the goal is most likely to be achieved over time through multiple iterations of confidential, developmental, multisource feedback events—linked to business-driven development planning—where development is rewarded and learning is valued. When individuals and organizations see that feedback doesn't kill; that information is being provided in service to learning; and that learning occurs through open, consistent feedback and the opportunity to practice needed skills; then we can all throw down our number 2 pencils.

This debate is about how to help people learn, grow, and change over time. I will argue that it is not done through ever-more-inventive rating systems that attempt to force distributions or foil the raters. It is not accomplished through punishment or public humiliation, by ignoring basic principles about the conditions under which people can accept and incorporate disconfirming information about the self. It is accomplished by thoughtful attention to creating environments where information is freely shared and accepted and where learning in service to individual and organizational goals is rewarded.

References

Carver, C. S., Scheier, M. F., & Weintraub, J. K. (1989). Assessing coping strategies: A theoretically based approach. *Journal of Personality and Social Psychology, 56*(2), 267-283.

Farh, J. L., Cannella, A. A., & Bedeian, A. G. (1991). Peer ratings, the impact of purpose on rating quality and user acceptance. *Group and Organizational Studies, 16*(4), 367-386.

Fleenor, J., McCauley, C., & Brutus, S. (1996). Self-other rating agreement and leader effectiveness. *Leadership Quarterly, 7*(4), 487-506.

Folkman, S., & Lazarus, R. S. (1985). If it changes it must be a process: Studies of emotion and coping during three stages of a college examination. *Journal of Personality and Social Psychology, 48,* 150-170.

Hazucha, J., Szymanski, C., & Birkeland, S. (1992). *Will my boss see my ratings? Effect of confidentiality on self-boss congruence.* Symposium of the American Psychological Association, Washington, D.C.

London, M., & Smither, J. W. (1996). *Can feedback change self-evaluations, skill development, and performance? Theory-based applications and directions for research.* Unpublished manuscript.

Meyer, H. H., Kaye, E., & French, J. R. P., Jr. (1965, January/February). Split roles in performance appraisal. *Harvard Business Review,* No. 65108, p. 123.

Raven, B. H., & Kruglanski, A. W. (1970). Conflict and power. In P. Swingle (Ed.), *The structure of conflict* (pp. 69-109). New York: Academic Press.

❦❦❦

Maxine A. Dalton is a research scientist and program manager at the Center for Creative Leadership, where she has trained hundreds of feedback specialists and given feedback to hundreds of individuals and groups since being introduced to the concept of 360-degree feedback in 1989. She has also been active in managing the process of the translation and adaptation of 360-degree-feedback instruments in other countries. Prior to coming to CCL, she was a consultant with Drake Beam Morin. Dalton's recent publications include "The Benefits of 360-degree Feedback for Organizations" in *Maximizing the Value of 360-degree Feedback: A Process for Successful Individual and Organizational Development* (Eds. W. Tornow, M. London, & CCL Associates; Jossey-Bass, March 1998); and with George P. Hollenbeck, *How to Design an Effective System for Developing Managers and Executives* (CCL, 1996). Dalton holds a Ph.D. in industrial/organizational psychology from the University of South Florida.

SOME FAULTY ASSUMPTIONS
THAT SUPPORT USING MULTI-RATER FEEDBACK
FOR PERFORMANCE APPRAISAL
Victoria A. Pollman

I believe in using 360-degree feedback strictly for development. It is supportive and promotes self-awareness. Using it for appraisal makes it punitive by its very nature. In fact, to do so is an artifact of an archaic, white-male-dominated management system that stresses command and control. It is antithetical to current leadership theory based on empowerment of employees. On its face it sounds very appealing to hold managers accountable and to give employees a say in their managers' ratings, but this approach is really built on a foundation of quicksand.

If you use 360-degree feedback for appraisal, the underlying philosophy supports the belief that you can force change. For development, its purpose is to enable change. When we, as managers, receive feedback that's used for (our) appraisal, (our) motivation the next time is to be *rated* as more effective, not necessarily to *be* more effective. If it's to be used strictly for our development, there's nothing in it for us other than to *be* a more effective manager.

And, finally, using 360-degree feedback for appraisal purposes is based on a "Theory X" philosophy that says we have to force our managers to change. Once again, it's the old command-and-control philosophy about managers: They're lazy and they're not going to change unless we bring out the club and hit them over the head with it at performance-appraisal time. Using 360-degree feedback for development is more of a "Theory Y" approach that says that people do care about being effective, and they're going to use data to be more effective.

Here are some assumptions for using 360-degree feedback for appraisal that haven't been closely examined and which I don't hold. Let's start with this assumption: Raters are going to be honest. What makes us think that just because we give somebody a form to fill out that he or she is going to be honest? In fact, in one study that Manny London did (London, Wohlers, & Gallagher, 1990), about a third of the raters said that they would give different answers if they weren't anonymous. So we know that we need anonymous raters if we're going to have any hope of getting accurate data. One of the assumptions is that raters will be honest, and I don't think that that's true.

The next assumption is that you can force people to change. Change is difficult even if it's something you recognize that you need to do. Even though you understand the need for change, and you accept it, it's still hard to do. If it weren't, I'd be exercising every day and weigh twenty-five pounds less. But can you *force* me to change? So far, no one's been able to. I don't think you can force people to change.

Another assumption that you have to make if you're using 360-degree feedback in an appraisal context is that improvement in scores represents real improvement on the job. Those with experience with 360-degree feedback know of examples where a manager's scores improved but the manager wasn't acting in the best interest of the organization. Or the scores decreased, apparently not getting better, but the manager was doing exactly what the organization wanted him or her to do. For example, what if you have low-performing members in a group and the manager starts taking action to address them? Well, how do you think those individuals who are not perform-ing very well think about this? Are they inclined to rate the manager higher and say, "Oh boy, this manager is a fair assessor of performance and listens to my point of view, and all the other kinds of things that we rate"? No. They give the manager lower scores, even though the manager is doing exactly what you want done.

Conversely, you could have a manager who received good scores and took actions completely contrary to what you want. Let's say something along the lines of, "Next week, they're going to be filling out the forms on me; I think we should cancel work. No work on Friday. Let's have a big picnic over at my house, and we'll put in a margarita machine." Maybe this is an exaggeration, but managers engage in activities to curry favor with their employees so they'll get higher ratings. And they may not be in the best interest of the organization at all. So just because scores go up doesn't mean real improvement occurs. And managers, of course, are more motivated to do these sorts of things if feedback is tied to performance appraisal.

Here's my favorite assumption that doesn't hold: Current performance-appraisal systems work adequately and will be improved with additional ratings. How many of you work in an organization where you have some kind of formal performance-appraisal system? (Almost all.) How many of you think that your formal performance-appraisal system works adequately? (Very few.) I rest my case! We've got terrible performance-appraisal systems, and what do we want to do? Take something that works beautifully—360-degree feedback—and tie it to a broken system!

Another assumption: You can design a management-control system that raters and ratees will not be able to manipulate to their advantage. Do any of you here have employees in your organization who haven't figured out how to manipulate any system you've come up with? I don't think so. They all can.

The last assumption is that the use of anonymous raters is legally practical. Wait until you get that in court! One of the central tenets of our judicial system is that the accused can confront his or her accusers. If I receive anonymous feedback and it's having a negative impact on my merit increase or chance of promotion, I'll say, "Let me see those raters. They're wrong. They didn't know me. They filled it out wrong. I want to talk to them." What happens when you respond, "I'm sorry we can't do that; they're anonymous." We may have lots of legal trouble with that one.

Reference

London, M., Wohlers, A. J., & Gallagher, P. (1990). 360-degree feedback surveys: A source of feedback to guide management development. *Journal of Management Development, 9*, 17-31.

☙☙☙

Victoria A. Pollman is general manager, human resources, at Texaco, where she manages the organization effectiveness function. She has also developed and implemented customized programs and integrated human resource systems, where she used the 360-degree-feedback process with individual leaders and intact management teams in the U.S. and overseas. In 1996, Pollman began a three-year loan assignment with Caltex, where she is responsible for designing human resource development systems and practices, including succession planning, high-potential identification and tracking, competency-model development, management/executive development, and employment and employee relations. A charter member of the Upward Feedback Forum, she holds a Ph.D. in industrial/organizational psychology from the University of Houston.

Maximizing the Uses of Multi-rater Feedback
David W. Bracken

Let me start by being clear about exactly what we are debating. Those of us on the "appraisal" or decision-making side of this argument certainly do not propose, nor have we ever proposed, taking the position that multi-rater feedback (MRF) is not a good developmental tool. I do believe that its very power is not maximized when used for development only, for reasons stated below. What we are debating is the position of the "development only" camp that it is never appropriate to use MRF for decision making, such as performance management or succession planning.

It would be too simple to refute the "development only" argument by simply pointing out that MRF for decision making has worked in many organizations, especially if we say that "worked" is synonymous with "survived." Certainly survival is one necessary but not sufficient requirement for success. The ultimate criterion for success is more likely defined as "sustained, targeted behavior change resulting in increased organization effectiveness."

We also need to know why MRF has flourished in some organizations and why it has died off in others. Timmreck and Bracken (1997) present research on twenty-seven MRF processes from a multi-rater consortium that had indicated implementation or planned implementation of MRF for decision making. This research, and others as well, has given us an initial list of critical factors necessary for successful (as defined above) MRF processes:

- Support from top management, including a long-term perspective on achieving results.
- Visible participation of top management.
- Validated, relevant competency (behavior, skill) model.
- Rater training.
- Rater accountability to provide honest feedback.
- Rater anonymity and confidentiality.
- Organization-wide implementation (for example, required participation).
- Easy-to-use feedback and report formats (that is, concise, clear, relevant).
- Ratee training on how to use results.
- Ratee feedback to raters and involvement of raters in action-planning.

- Ratee accountability for action-planning and follow-through.
- Training of the managers of ratees on appropriate use of MRF.
- Development resources provided by the organization.

All of the above factors may be necessary for a "successful" MRF implementation; much like a multiplicative equation, if any variable goes to zero, the total result goes to zero as well. Some of our adversaries actually point to the Timmreck and Bracken (1997) research to highlight that some decision-making MRF systems (about half of those studied) have indeed "died," leading to a true "half full, half empty" view of the results. To them I would offer two observations: (1) Some, if not most, of the "deaths" can be attributed to either missing critical factors (such as those listed above) or extraneous events (for instance, elimination of pay raises) that made the feedback moot; (2) Where is the parallel research on the effectiveness of "development only" processes? Yours may be the real glass house.

Looking at my list of critical factors, I would propose that decision-making MRF processes are much more likely to satisfy these criteria than are the development-only processes. The prototypical development-only system often has different characteristics, such as:

- Voluntary participation, either by self-nomination or in conjunction with some development experience (for example, a management development course).
- A generic (off-the-shelf) competency model, sometimes of considerable length (over 100 items).
- Little, if any, communication of top-management support.
- No rater training or accountability.
- No ratee accountability for action-planning or development.
- No expectations for the managers of ratees to help use results.
- No tie to other systems that support and reinforce ongoing behavior change.

The development-only proponents may even point out that these characteristics create a "nonthreatening" environment where raters are more apt to provide honest feedback and ratees are more open to self-reflection and change. The first point regarding rater honesty will be addressed below. As for the probability of behavior change under this scenario, we can point to results such as those published by Hezlett and Ronnkvist (1996) that suggest that, without required action-planning and feedback to raters, the probability of observed behavior change is very low. How likely is it, then, that organization effectiveness will be improved if only some employees participate (on an irregular basis), and, of those, only some will follow the recommended steps that are likely to result in behavior change, especially if the desired behaviors are not sustained by a culture and systems communicated in sync with the feedback?

I believe that MRF used for development only is, at best, a waste of time and money. A few souls will use the information for self-development and achieve the desired results; as many (or more) will ignore the feedback and go on their merry way. More nefarious outcomes might include a focus on irrelevant competencies (that is, not customized to the organization's strategies) or an undermining of future MRF efforts as participants grow wary of the benefits of MRF when no behavior change or accountability is observed.

The most compelling argument for the use of MRF in support of performance appraisals is the opportunity to improve, even incrementally, the quality of a process that is found lacking in most organizations. I shudder to think where society would be if we followed Dr. Pollman's (and Dr. Deming's?) advice and simply throw out everything that doesn't work perfectly. True, most performance-management systems don't "work" and therefore need to be fixed. MRF should be a major tool in our toolkit.

In their book *Understanding Performance Appraisal*, Murphy and Cleveland (1995) make the following statement: "In the future we expect that performance appraisals will routinely incorporate information from multiple sources, and that peer input will be the most important source of performance appraisal information" (p. 373).

It is truly inevitable that feedback from sources other than the supervisor will become part of our performance-management systems. The following propositions are offered as some of the reasoning for this inevitability:

1. *Feedback helps improve performance, under certain conditions.* These conditions include the need for the feedback to be specific, relevant, timely, constructive, and credible.

2. *Supervisors are in progressively worsening positions to provide quality feedback.* In most organizations, supervisors (if they exist at all) are managing larger groups, that is, with larger spans of control. This affects both opportunity to observe and opportunity to provide quality feedback. To compound the problem, the increasing use of teams often requires that employees make their most significant contributions in settings where the supervisor has no opportunity to directly observe performance whatsoever.

3. *Supervisors never were very good sources of feedback.* The supervisor as the sole source of feedback in the classic appraisal situation often has had little motivation to provide quality feedback. There is little reward in confronting the performance "problem" and often little incentive to pass it on to the employee. Supervisors often do not have the skills required for good feedback, although some organizations have made good-faith efforts to provide training in this arena. Performance appraisals have historically been looked at as a human-resources administrative exercise that is not tied to real business priorities.

4. *There are other sources of quality feedback (that is, peers, direct reports, customers, team members).* Forty years of research has shown that co-workers can provide reliable, valid, and unique perspectives on an individual's performance.

If we look at a simple model of performance—Performance = Ability x Opportunity x Motivation—and apply it to an MRF context, we know that ability is the least of our worries. Co-workers can (and do) reliably observe behaviors. With training, we can improve their performance by having them focus on job-relevant behaviors, addressing the gremlins of ratings such as halo, leniency, severity, attribution, recentness, and so on.

As for opportunity, the primary argument for using co-workers (and sometimes customers) for feedback is their very proximity to the employee. We can further improve this situation in the MRF process by including rules and guidelines for sufficient "opportunity to observe" in the feedback process.

The motivation of raters to provide honest, accurate, reliable feedback is at the very center of this debate. It may be the single major obstacle in the eyes of the development-only camp. There is published research that does indeed suggest that MRF used for decision making results in more lenient ratings, which are in turn deemed to be less honest (although we really don't know which are more accurate or how far from accurate they are). This lack of honesty is attributed to fears on the part of raters that their honest feedback will result in (1) some negative consequences for the ratee for which they might feel guilty or (2) discovery of their ratings by the ratee, who will seek some kind of revenge. In actuality, both of these fears probably exist in development-only systems as well, but arguably to a reduced extent.

Are there solutions to the "motivation problem," or should we admit defeat and abandon MRF for decision making? The fact (and it is a fact) that MRF has succeeded in some organizations when used for decision making would strongly suggest that there are solutions to this problem. I offer a few here:

1. *Hold raters accountable.* Edwards and Ewen (1996) would say that this is the sine qua non of MRF for decision making. Rater accountability basically asks raters to provide honest feedback. "Dishonest" feedback shows invalid response patterns, such as selecting the same value repeatedly for every (or almost every) rating. There are two basic requirements for rater accountability. First, raters cannot be totally anonymous if we are to track down abusers. (What we do with invalid ratings is another decision.) Second, it must be clearly communicated to raters that they will be held accountable for quality feedback (as supervisors have traditionally been held accountable) and what the consequences (if any) will be.

2. *Make raters part of the solution.* To the extent that raters become partners in using the output of their feedback, we could reasonably expect increased motivation to provide honest feedback. The most typical example is to have raters participate in the analysis of the ratee's results to create recommended development plans. This participation can take on many different forms but ultimately shows the raters that their honest feedback can have impact, and that dishonest feedback is a waste of everyone's time and resources.

3. *Hold ratees accountable for action and follow-through.* Raters can only be expected to be full participants in the MRF process if they feel that their input is being used in the manner intended.

4. *Tie MRF content and processes to other business systems.* As a stand-alone process, MRF will have little value to the participants, raters, and ratees alike. Yes, some ratees will take the feedback to heart and do the "right" thing. As noted earlier, these cases will be the minority unless some business relevance is established. Ultimately, top management will not support the resources devoted to an "unaligned" system.

5. *Give MRF similar stature to other business-measurement systems.* In the "balanced scorecard" approach to performance management, significant measurements are created to reflect the priorities of the organization. Historically, many of these measures have been quantitative and results-oriented. Organizations are rapidly incorporating more qualitative measures into the balanced scorecard, such as customer satisfaction. MRF, as a measure of "how" the results are achieved, is also being integrated into measurement systems, often starting with senior management and working its way down the organization.

6. *Create a method for discovering "abusers."* Rater abuse was discussed above in terms of rater accountability, and positive accountability for ratees takes the form of required action-planning. We must also hold ratees

accountable by discouraging inappropriate behavior in the MRF context. Through anonymous 800 lines or ombudsmen-type positions, employers must be able to identify ratees who exhibit behaviors such as attempting to directly influence ratings; trying to identify sources of specific ratings; threatening negative consequences for low raters; or violating any expressed rule or guideline for the MRF process.

Some of these recommendations do sound a little like "Theory X," especially the "accountability" part. But London, Smither, and Adsit (1997) have a compelling argument for the future of MRF processes and the role of accountability. They propose that accountability comes from three sources: the rater, the ratee, and the organization. In order to make MRF work, all of these parties must be held accountable for fulfilling their role. I suggest that if the organization is not willing to establish and enforce accountabilities, then MRF is probably not worth the effort and expense. In those organizations, MRF will be correctly characterized as a "fad" and should die a timely death. I would go so far as to say that if organizations are not willing to endorse use of MRF for decision making, then maybe a rapid death is preferred to a slow one.

A metaphor may best sum up our position, as dangerous as metaphors may be. MRF for development is something like an electric car. Electric cars are not a bad idea in themselves and do no harm (although considerable investments continue to be made, with questionable progress). They also will do little good in addressing their main purpose—improving the environment—until they are used by large numbers of drivers. This is unlikely to happen until they are improved and, eventually, users are held accountable for using them. Until that day, we search for and implement ways to make gasoline-powered cars more efficient and environmentally friendly, coupled with accountability (for instance, inspections). This route is having a much more substantial positive impact on the environment while it satisfies the needs of users. Going back to our view of the most compelling argument for using MRF, achieving small incremental changes across large numbers of users is having substantial positive impact on our environment with an imperfect solution.

References

Edwards, M. R., & Ewen, A. J. (1996). *360-degree feedback.* New York: American Management Association.

Hezlett, S. A., & Ronnkvist, A. M. (1996, April). *The effects of multi-rater feedback on managers' skill development: Factors influencing behavior change.* Paper presented at the Eleventh Annual Conference of the Society for Industrial and Organizational Psychology, San Diego, CA.

London, M., Smither, J. W., & Adsit, D. J. (1997, June). Accountability: The Achilles' heel of multi-source feedback. *Group & Organization Management, 22*(2), 162-184.

Murphy, K. R., & Cleveland, J. N. (1995). *Understanding performance appraisal.* Thousand Oaks, CA: Sage Publications.

Timmreck, C. W., & Bracken, D. W. (1997, Spring). Multisource feedback: A study of its use in decision making. *Employment Relations Today,* pp. 21-27.

❧❧❧

David W. Bracken is president of dwb assessments, inc., where he specializes in the development and implementation of large-scale, multi-source feedback systems. He is also co-founder of the Upward Feedback Forum. Previously, he was affiliated with William M. Mercer, Inc.; Towers Perrin; and Personnel Decisions, Inc. His recent publications include "Straight Talk About Multirater Feedback" in *Training and Development* (September, 1994) and "Multisource (360-Degree) Feedback: Surveys for Individual and Organizational Development" in *Organizational Surveys* (1996; A. I. Kraut, Ed.). Bracken holds a Ph.D. degree from Georgia Tech in industrial/organizational psychology and is a licensed psychologist in the state of Georgia.

FITTING MULTI-RATER FEEDBACK INTO ORGANIZATIONAL STRATEGY

Robert A. Jako

If you want to learn about the culture of an organization, look at what it pays for. To argue that multi-rater feedback (MRF) should *never* be paid for is a classically conservative stance, namely, that we know of one or two virtues coming from an existing entity and we don't want to consider expanding on them. Holding to such a position will ultimately result in MRF's dying a slow death, with no linkage to what drives organizational success.

The vast majority of organizations using MRF have implemented it by *not* connecting it to managerial decisions on pay or promotion. This is beginning to change, but most indications are that the changes are coming about due to a demand from the decision-makers for the data, rather than from an informed and logical strategy. A Corporate Leadership Council study in late 1995 showed eighty percent of benchmarked companies were using MRF as their primary performance-management tool. All used an indirect strategy, leaving the ultimate determination of pay to the manager of the position. Thus, it seems clear that there is a functional need, which is being acted on, for an integrated approach to performance management. A constructive response to this movement is to explore how to make it work for organizations, rather than to lament its methodological shortcomings from an ivory tower. This paper explores some of the strategic foundations of the movement we are observing.

Why do businesses advocate and invest in performance development, and why do they endeavor to pay for performance differentially at the individual level? They invest to get increased performance from the same employee, and they pay for performance because individuals exhibit differing levels of performance that lend themselves respectively to organizational outcomes. There is a within-persons and between-persons contrast in the methods and goals, but in the final analysis the entity being addressed is, in employees' and managers' perceptions, singular: performance. MRF is often implemented in such a way as to communicate that there are two different performances floating around in the organization—one that we pay for and one that we don't. The really disturbing part of this from an organizational standpoint is that the one that we don't pay for is the one we are methodologically preaching to be the "true" measure of performance.

One of the anchoring statements made by those who would prefer to keep MRF out of the performance-management arena is that feedback is only honest if the respondents are assured that no one but the ratee will see the results. In other words, "I'll communicate about performance but only under certain circumstances." This is a position that we need to engage but not one to which we should necessarily concede. Work is transitioning to being team-based. Communication about performance has always been a business responsibility, as part of working with people toward a common goal. But today's flatter structures, increased numbers of peers, and reliance on shared understandings virtually make communication a product.

Although organizations need to reinforce the notion that communication about performance is a business accountability, insulating the feedback process from the operational currency of the organization and keeping measured results secret from the manager symbolizes a contradictory philosophy. Team members and leaders need to know each other's strengths as well as weaknesses in order to capitalize on the group's collective talent and knowledge. In the long run, MRF could facilitate a shared understanding in very much the same way that we see teams go through start-ups, but in an ongoing manner as part of how the business operates. In the short run, it seems a viable first step to make the team leader aware of how people can work together efficiently. Isolating MRF as an anonymous measurement, devoid of any visible link to operations, denies team members the opportunity to fully leverage their team's potential.

Organizations are focusing on the customer more than ever before. Learning about customers and what they want, through surveys and focus groups, is logically responded to with changes in products, distribution channels, service delivery, and even personnel. While organizations try to communicate this philosophy to their employee populations, they contradict it by not demonstrating an internal business accountability for responding to MRF. Not linking results to pay sends the message that responding to internal customers is optional and not connected to improved business performance. Communication is a two-way process, yet without accountability for responding to the data, MRF becomes a measurement without a cause.

There is a troubling "Theory X" assumption embedded in the argument not to link MRF to decision making. Arguing for the segregation of MRF from performance management is to suggest that feedback providers will never trust their manager's ability to effectively use the data in relation to pay *and* development, and that they will never be comfortable with the ability to actually direct organizational resources based on their perceptions of their peers' performance. The manager's job is to develop, coach, and evaluate his or her reports. By not allowing access to the data, we are communicating explicitly that he or she cannot do these things effectively. To argue (as some seem to) that this state of affairs is sound and must endure is to suggest that managers will never be able to achieve this level of competence and employees this level of empowerment.

Perhaps it would be more constructive to frame the problem that currently exists rather than cast such broad proclamations of doom over our managerial ranks. Avoiding the link between developing and paying for performance should be seen as an implementation strategy rather than a philosophical position. We readily agree that many work environments have cultures that would readily substantiate all of the "Theory X" predictions regarding an integrated approach to performance management. But it is shortsighted to say "no" to a whole line of progress toward an environment in which we understand our performance and its fit into the organization's strategic functioning through fully informed engagements with our managers.

Rather than concede to an assumption that all work environments are fraught with distrust and cannot change, let's focus on the real challenge: protecting the integrity of the data. The implementation issue rests in methodology and a concern that we not contaminate the upward/peer perspectives with layers of concerns about relationships, pay, and longevity. There are many possible approaches to managing the fidelity of the data, as demonstrated by Dave Bracken's thoughtful list. There are also some approaches to incorporating the culture in which you are working into the implementation process, to eliminate the argument over whether "Theory X" or "Theory Y" applies.

For example, leave the decision to link MRF to pay up to the recipients, at the point at which they realize the integrity of the data relies on their honest and forthcoming participation. If a participative group opts for a link in an informed manner, it implies that they appreciate the fidelity of the data and what kinds of rating behaviors are necessary to sustain the fidelity. We know this can happen. There have been a number of cited instances in which this practice was largely successful. I have seen departments within my own organization successfully work with this approach.

Another option is to implement your MRF with the linkage as a stated goal but let the local work group design how that goal is achieved. In other words, let employees ask themselves the question, "What kinds of peer perceptions am I willing to let drive my pay, and to what degree?" If employees feel they have control over the implementation process, there is a much higher probability that they will trust it and use it constructively.

Citing one instance of success is sufficient to disprove the claim that linking MRF to performance management will necessarily lead to the corruption of the virtues of MRF. This has clearly been done. While there are plenty of instances in which linking MRF to decision making would not be advisable, it is simply irresponsible for a scientific community to shut the door on pursuing performance feedback that is *relevant,* as well as valid. Relevance is what will define whether MRF is a valid part of an organization's function.

❦ ❦ ❦

Robert A. Jako manages Physician Performance Assessment and Compensation, which is charged with development and implementation of performance and compensation improvement for The Permanente Medical Group. He is responsible for developing tools and measures that enable physician managers to effectively link individual and team performance to the organization's strategic direction, which includes such projects as developing performance feedback systems for physicians and creating self-guided 360-degree-feedback tools for managers. He also participates in the design of executive incentive plans for the medical group as well as partner organizations within the Kaiser Permanente Program. Jako holds a Ph.D. in industrial/organizational psychology from Colorado State University.

On Choosing Sides: Seeing the Good in Both
Cynthia D. McCauley

I attended the debate where Dalton, Pollman, Bracken, and Jako presented their views on whether 360-degree assessments should be used only for feedback and development or whether these types of assessments are also appropriate for use in administrative decision-making. At the end of that debate, they asked the audience to take sides. If we agreed with the feedback-for-development-only view, then we were to move to one side of the room. If we agreed that multi-rater assessments should also be used for administrative decision-making, we were to move to the other side. At the end of a heated debate, the debaters wanted some evidence of who had won. Audience opinion seemed a good source of evidence.

However, after hearing four people with a wealth of experience on the topic, I found myself not being able to take one side or the other. I ended up standing in the middle of the room. But the debaters would have none of that! I was told I had to choose. This was very disconcerting. First, both sides had presented what seemed to me to be quite logical arguments for their case. But I was not sure the cases were directly comparable; in other words, I wasn't sure they were always talking about the same thing. Second, each of the debaters aroused negative emotions in me because of some of the assumptions about human nature and organizational life that seemed to be behind their positions. Each of them made me feel that working inside an organization was pretty horrible. Taking sides would be like choosing between two evils. Finally, I did not have the depth of experience with 360-degree assessments that the debaters did; thus, I did not have a strong framework to use to organize the large amount of information they were throwing at me.

So I wasn't ready to make a decision about which side I was on. I wasn't even sure there were opposite sides to choose between. What this debate did do for me was to stimulate me to think more carefully about the issues the debaters were putting on the table. And isn't this what a good debate is supposed to do? After struggling through my own thoughts, I was surprised to find myself choosing the middle ground again but this time for different reasons—not because I was confused, or not attracted to the views of organizations expressed by each side, or lacked the experiences to decide who was right, but because I see value in multiple uses of 360-degree assessments.

I do think that there is an important place in organizational life for in-depth, confidential 360-degree feedback and that if this feedback is provided in the right context it can be an important stimulus for individual change. I also think that 360-degree assessments can make for better administrative decisions about individuals—decisions that can motivate people to change; but here again, the contextual factors can make or break such uses of 360-degree assessments.

In what follows, I'll describe how I came to these conclusions—what in the various positions presented by the debaters I found troubling and what I found stimulating, what common themes I found in all the viewpoints, and the emerging framework that helped me make sense of the debate for myself. I do not claim to have found the answer to this debate. I'm sure there are factors and issues I have yet to consider. But for the time being, I have found *my* answer—one that I feel comfortable testing out as I move forward. What I hope this chapter will do is stimulate your own efforts to make sense of the conflicting points of view presented by the debaters. My clear bias is that you end up with a position that is integrative, one that is less polarized than those presented by the debaters (who I presume tended to present more extreme positions to accentuate the points they were trying to make).

The Viewpoints

Let me begin with how I understood and interpreted each of the viewpoints.

Maxine Dalton is clearly focused on how 360-degree assessments can be used to help individuals learn, grow, and change over time. She posits that for these assessments to have this desired outcome, they need to be based on high-quality data (that is, honest ratings) and be fed back to the individual in a way that he or she can hear and accept the data. To ensure honest ratings, raters need to feel that their ratings are anonymous and that the data will be shared confidentially with the person being assessed. Likewise, confidentiality is an important prerequisite for creating the safe environment a person needs for hearing and accepting the data. She argues that using the 360-degree data for administrative decision-making would violate the conditions needed for honest ratings and a safe environment.

What I feel Dalton is saying is that if we are to make feedback a humane process (and thus one people will respond to), we must take it out of the inhumane context of the modern organization. In the organizational picture she paints, people cannot be honest with one another in terms of what they think about each other's strengths and weaknesses. They fear that honest feedback will make the other person feel bad, or if that person has more power, he or she will level some retribution toward them. Thus they will provide honest feedback only if the recipient will not know who said what.

In this scenario, providing upward feedback appears to be particularly risky because people with power cannot be trusted to not misuse their power. To me, this is a bleak view of the regard people have for one another in the modern organization—a view that certainly has some basis in reality but surely isn't that bad in all organizations. Dalton seemed to be responding to the worst-case scenario within organizations. However, toward the end of her presentation, she did give me hope that formal 360-degree assessment and feedback could be a tool to help move organizations toward cultures where negative feedback would not always engender defensive reactions. This does create a challenging dilemma: How can a process that is conducted independent of the normal operations of an organization have an impact on those operations?

Vicki Pollman makes a more pointed attack against using 360-degree assessments in administrative decisions. Whereas Dalton builds the case for why these assessments should be used only in a confidential development process, Pollman focuses more on why they should not be used in one particular administrative process—performance appraisals. She finds fault in the assumptions behind using 360-degree assessments for performance appraisal (raters will be honest, people can be forced to change, improvement in ratings represents real improvement on the job). And then, of course, the real jab: Why add 360-degree assessments to an administrative process that doesn't work as a mechanism for changing behavior anyway?

Pollman presents an even darker view of organizations than Dalton does: a system that is bent on keeping people in line, evaluating people for the sole purpose of finding out what they are not doing right, using only punitive measures as motivators. In her scenario, organizations are populated by people who are highly motivated to manipulate their ratings and by employees who are gullible enough to fall for this sort of manipulation. Although this view of organizations does seem extreme to me, it certainly highlights some important factors that have to be confronted to prevent the abuse of the 360-degree assessment processes.

David Bracken focuses on how 360-degree assessments can be used to foster "systematic, targeted behavior change resulting in increased organizational effectiveness." To achieve this result, he argues that 360-degree assessments need to be used for administrative decision-making in addition to their use in feedback for development. He clarifies that the debate is not between using 360-degree assessments for development versus administrative decision-making, but rather between development-only uses versus development plus decision making.

He points out the conditions that are present when 360-degree assessments survive in organizations (for instance, top-management support and participation, relevant competency models, organization-wide implementation) and argues that confidential, development-only feedback processes often don't meet these conditions. Just as Dalton appears to resist using 360-degree assessments for administrative decision-making because of what could happen in the worst-case scenarios, Bracken seems to resist development-only uses in part because of what these uses don't do when they are poorly designed. All the factors that he lists as missing in most development-only uses of 360-degree assessment don't have to be missing from them.

As expected, Bracken does not have a dark view of organizations. He does, however, present organizations as very rational places: If all the systems are in place and people are trained to do the right thing, then everything will work in a logical and fair way. He also doesn't express much confidence in people's ability to absorb feedback and change on their own. Just as the dark views of organizations gave me pause, this "rational organization/irrational man" view took me aback.

Robert Jako argues that 360-degree assessments will not survive if they are not linked to an organization's pay system because rewards determine behavior. Thus, like Bracken, he emphasizes the primacy of external rewards on changing individuals' behavior. He also uses another line of reasoning that Bracken begins and is expanded upon here: Work is changing (becoming more team-based and customer-focused) in ways that require inputs from multiple points of view in order to make good administrative decisions about people. The manager no longer has all the knowledge needed to make these decisions on his or her own. Jako argues that to not give managers access to this information denies them the ability to do their jobs in a responsible manner.

Jako also came across as having a rational view of organizations, with a heavy emphasis on the central importance of rewards in general and pay in particular in determining behavior—a position that is often the focus of lively debates. Organizations often have trouble implementing pay systems that actually reward what they say they want to reward. Jako's viewpoint also seemed driven by pragmatism more so than any of the other debaters.

The Differences and Commonalities

Although the debaters state it in various ways, the central issue being debated is whether 360-degree assessments should be used in administrative decision-making. Dalton and Pollman take the position that 360-degree assessments should *never* be linked to administrative decision-making. Bracken and Jako take the position that 360-degree assessments should *always* be linked to administrative decision-making. What are the different assumptions and frameworks at work in these two major points of view?

The first obvious difference is that the feedback-for-development-only side believes in the primacy of internal motivation, while the need-to-use-in-administrative-decisions side believes in the primacy of external motivation. I tend to be biased in the internal motivation direction, too, but it was actually Pollman's comments that made me see clearly the importance of external motivators (although I do not think she intended to do so). In arguing that you can't force people to change, she says that even if you understand what kind of change is needed and accept the need for change, you don't always do what you need to do to make the change happen.

The example she gives (that many people can identify with) is the struggle to lose weight. Bracken and Jako would probably reply that the reason you do not lose weight even though you want to, you know you should, and you even know the steps that would get you there is because there are no external, immediate consequences for your not losing weight. If your job (for instance, acting or modeling) depended on it, you might be more motivated. If your doctor said your health would deteriorate rapidly in the next six months because of your excess weight, you might be motivated. If somebody said they would give you lots of money for losing it, you might be motivated. I'm reminded of an example from my own experience. I never wore a seatbelt until a state law provided me with the motivation—despite the fact that I knew it was better for me to wear it and I certainly knew how to operate the mechanism!

One of the reasons that the development-only debaters put more emphasis on internal motivation and the administrative-use debaters put more emphasis on external motivation is because they may be working to achieve different kinds of changes in individuals. Dalton talks about learning, growth, and change over time whereas Bracken refers to targeted behavioral change in service of organizational effectiveness. Dalton is speaking of learning that "sticks" with the person as he or she moves to new situations and contexts, of growth that reflects new understanding and broader capacities. Bracken is speaking of specific changes in behavior that make the individual more effective in his or her current context. Take the example of losing weight. If you need to lose weight to be effective in your current situation and you engage in the behaviors (that is, increased exercise, eating less) that lead to decreased weight, then you have likely met the criteria of change that increases current effectiveness. External motivators can be very effective in this context. To meet the criterion of learning and growth, you would need to have adopted a lifestyle that incorporates the changed behaviors on an ongoing basis and have a concept of self as one who naturally engages in these behaviors for your own satisfaction.

Another difference in the development-only versus the administrative-use camps is the political versus rational view of organizations. I pointed out these differences when I reviewed the viewpoints above, so I won't go into detail again here. There are several consequences of these different lenses that do seem to affect the tacks the debaters took. Those using the political lens tend to focus on not using 360-degree assessment for administrative purposes because of what current organizations are like. Those using the rational lens admit that current organizational cultures aren't all that they should be but express optimism that they could improve and that 360-degree assessments are part of the process for improving them. Although not directly stated, I sensed that those with the political lens feared the fragility of the human ego (for example, defensiveness, denial of negative feedback, retaliation against threats) whereas those with the rational lens feared the fragility of the human will (for example, inability to change without some push from the organization).

Despite these differences, I also found some common ground. Both sides started from the premise that getting evaluations of skills, competencies, or behaviors from superiors, peers, and subordinates was a useful assessment technique. From each perspective, 360-degree assessments resulted in useful data—they disagreed, however, on how that data is best used to motivate change.

A main reason that each side objected to the other side's point of view was that the right context couldn't be created to use 360-degree assessments in the way the other side was advocating. If 360-degree assessments were available for administrative decisions, managers would misuse the data, ratings would be manipulated, and raters could not be counted on to be honest, and so forth. If 360-degree assessments were available only to the individual for his or her own development, raters and ratees would not be accountable, the organization might send mixed messages about what's important, and so forth. At least both sides seemed to agree that the context surrounding the use of 360-degree assessments was important.

Finally, they all pointed out that getting honest assessments from raters is an issue, and that this issue seemed to be bigger when using the assessments for administrative decisions than when using them in confidential feedback. There are several reasons why people may not be honest in their evaluations of another person: guilt that negative evaluations will make someone feel bad, worry that the other person will dislike us for having a negative opinion about him or her (and thus harm our working relationship), fear that the other person will directly harm us in some retaliative act, and not wanting to feel responsible for the decisions that might be made based on our evaluations. The first reason will exist whether the feedback is anonymous or not. The next two reasons are mitigated if feedback is anonymous; the last reason, if the data are not used for administrative decisions. The easiest way to get honest ratings seems to be to make them anonymous and confidential. One of the biggest obstacles for those who want to use 360-degree evaluations for administrative purposes, then, is how to eliminate the factors contributing to less honest feedback.

Where I End Up: Different Purposes Require Different Contexts and Processes

I see merits on each side of this debate. I am left convinced that 360-degree assessments can be useful inputs to administrative decisions. In many organizations, managers would be foolish to rely only on their own assessments in making administrative decisions about the people who report to them; they do not have the opportunity to observe many of the skills and behaviors they need to assess, and they cannot know what it is like to be these people's peers, customers, or subordinates. I also think that any organization that is moving toward more distributed or empowered decision-making processes is not being true to that vision if it continues to use a strongly hierarchical process for making decisions about pay, promotions, or job assignments. Although Pollman sees linking 360-degree assessments to administrative decisions as a command-and-control tactic, I see it as just the opposite—an opportunity for employees to have a voice in who gets rewarded.

At the same time, I am convinced that confidential feedback is a necessary ingredient for personal development. Individuals do need safe environments to take a hard look at themselves, to reflect on who they could become, to take stock of their situation. Co-workers also need the occasional opportunity to give feedback only to the recipient without worrying about what the organizational implications for the individual might be. It's a necessary ingredient in building the kind of supportive relationships we seek in our worklife.

In other words, my view is that 360-degree assessments do not need to *always* be linked to administrative decisions, nor do they *always* need to be decoupled from them. But the processes and contexts to ensure good administrative decisions and those to ensure good feedback for development appear to be quite different. I don't believe the same 360-degree-assessment process can serve both purposes well.

Instead of debating the best way to use 360-degree assessments, I want to look more closely at (1) the circumstances that contribute to successful use of 360-degree assessments in administrative decision-making and those that contribute to successful use of these assessments in feedback for development, and (2) how the assessment process itself may differ depending on how the data will be used.

But I first want to argue that, although they may share an overlapping goal of shaping and changing behaviors in the workplace, administrative decision-making and feedback have additional goals. I think it is important to keep these additional goals in mind as we examine when and how to use 360-degree assessments in administrative decision-making and in feedback (see the figure below).

By "administrative decisions about individuals," I mean decisions about what jobs to give individuals, how and how much to reward them, and what kind of support they need. (I don't consider performance appraisals administrative decision-making, although they can be tools in administrative decisions.) Getting individuals to change ineffective behaviors is only one factor

---

Goals of Administrative Decision-making and Feedback

Administrative Decisions about Individuals

• Change behaviors of employees

• Clarify/reinforce norms

• Optimize human resources

Feedback to Individuals

• Change behaviors of employees

• Understand self

• Clarify expectations and perceptions among co-workers

---

driving decisions about pay, promotions, reprimands, job assignments, and training opportunities. Decision-makers are also trying to optimize their human resources by matching people to jobs that leverage their strengths, to sustain good performance and clarify organizational norms by rewarding positive behaviors and outcomes, and to keep growing talent through challenging assignments and access to formal training-and-development programs. All of these decisions require the manager to have a good sense of the individual's strengths and weaknesses.

Likewise, encouraging individuals to change is only one reason why an organization might offer its employees confidential feedback. Many assessment-for-development programs would consider themselves successful if individuals receiving feedback gain a clearer sense of themselves—their strengths, their weaknesses, what makes them tick, where they want to be headed in life. As results of the feedback, observers may not see clear changes in behavior but rather an increased self-confidence, a clearer sense of direction, and a focusing of strengths on tasks where they are needed. These individuals have experienced something more akin to renewal than change.

Another reason for feedback is to clarify expectations and perceptions among people who work closely together. Participants who receive 360-degree feedback can sometimes get messages from their raters that are confusing to them. They are encouraged by feedback facilitators to use the feedback as the beginning of a conversation with the raters, to try to better understand the message the raters are giving. Sometimes these conversations lead to the surfacing of misunderstandings and differences in viewpoints. A better working relationship can emerge from these conversations—with or without behavioral changes on the part of either party.

Contexts and Processes

Because administrative decisions and feedback have different goals (beyond their shared goal of creating change in individuals), because they rely on different mechanisms for motivating change, and because raters apparently respond differently to these two different uses of 360-degree data, different contexts and processes are needed.

I think of *context* as both the immediate context surrounding the 360-degree assessment and the larger organizational culture. My hypothesis is that 360-degree assessments for confidential feedback will work to the degree that the organizational culture values personal development and self-understanding. Ideally, such a culture is reflected in employees seeking opportunities to stretch and grow in the workplace, in bosses viewing employee development as one of their core responsibilities, and in systems for the creation and implementation of development plans. In these organizations, individual differences (for instance, how people approach problems, their interaction styles, and their preferences for certain tasks) are recognized and celebrated, and the conflicts these differences can give rise to are openly examined and continuously negotiated.

This culture translates to a 360-degree assessment-for-development context with two key ingredients: feedback facilitators and implemented development plans. Feedback facilitators help recipients make sense of their data. They point out patterns or themes; they help connect the data with other ways the individual understands him- or herself (for instance, personality profiles, preferences, current challenges, past experiences); they gently prod the individual to look at aspects of the data that are less pleasant. Feedback facilitators might help recipients begin thinking about development plans suggested by the feedback, but these plans need to be finalized with the stakeholders back in the organization who are affected by the changes put forth in the plan. These stakeholders then need to support and hold the recipient accountable for implementing the development plans. If 360-degree assessments for confidential feedback are events unconnected to individuals' evolving ways of understanding themselves or to the realities and stakeholders back in the workplace, then they are unlikely to live up to their developmental promise.

Likewise, my hypothesis is that 360-degree assessment for administrative decisions will work to the degree that the organizational culture supports the widespread sharing of information (up, down, and laterally) and employee involvement in decision making. If the organization tightly controls access to information, if all decision making is clearly top-down, and if management has a command-and-control view of organizations, then I would agree with Dalton and Pollman that 360-degree assessment for administrative decisions could be disastrous. Asking for participation from employees only when other employees are being evaluated would likely create suspicion and distrust.

Thus, in order to foster the kind of 360-degree-assessment process that employees are willing to make work, they need to have a clear understanding of the kinds of decisions their input is being sought for and see that the information they provide is indeed taken seriously and considered in the decision-making process. If it is tied to a performance-appraisal process that they know doesn't mean much in the long run, or if the boss always makes the call the way he or she sees it regardless of input from others, then there is little incentive for creating and sharing assessment data about others.

I once had a conversation with an executive at a conference on executive selection. He said that he had committed to a shared decision-making model around selection decisions for positions on his immediate staff. He admitted to having been overruled on a couple of occasions, but the decisions turned out to be good ones. I remember thinking that I would have to take the task of assessing the strengths and weaknesses of potential candidates a lot more seriously if I worked with this executive.

In addition to context, the process itself—what kind of data is collected in what way—is an important aspect of 360-degree assessments that needs to be designed to fit the use. Whereas the cultures that support different uses may overlap or at least not be mutually exclusive, the processes that support confidential feedback for development and administrative decision-making may look quite different. There are probably a number of dimensions along which the process may differ depending on the use, but the two that stood out for me were (1) breadth of data and (2) the importance of "accuracy."

If the goal of the 360-degree-assessment process is self-understanding and personal development, then the process needs to be designed so that the individual gets a broad, well-rounded, in-depth view of his or her strengths and weaknesses. Such a process would have a number of the following characteristics:

• The assessment instrument would cast a broad net—a wide range of skills, behaviors, and mandates would be included.

• Data from a broad range of people would be sought, including people who have a close working or personal relationship with the ratee and those who experience the individual more from a distance.

• Raters would be able to communicate two kinds of "low" ratings: viewing the ratee as (1) having had the opportunity to show competence but falling short in that demonstration (for instance, a weakness) or (2) not having had the opportunity to show competence (for instance, an untested area).

• Self-ratings would be an important part of the process so that the ratee can compare his or her own view with those of others.

• Other self-assessment data (for example, personality, preferences, values) would be collected at the same time to help the ratee better understand how his or her own psychological makeup influences how others experience him or her.

If the goal of the 360-degree-assessment process is to provide input into administrative decision-making, then the data should focus on what is most needed for those decisions. For example:

• Ratings on every dimension of performance may not be necessary; rather, areas where an individual particularly excels or stumbles may be the most important information.

• The dimensions used in the assessment instrument may need to be customized for particular jobs or levels.

• Data-collection instruments may need to be short so that a number of people could be rated at the same time by the same raters.

• Ratings on overall dimensions may be more important than ratings on a long list of items.

• Rather than being a key comparison point, self-ratings would be collected as another source of data to feed into decision making.

Finally, the two uses may call for two different mind-sets from the raters. Much has been said by the debaters about the importance of honesty from raters. Honesty seems particularly important in the context of feedback for development, where getting a better sense of how one is experienced by other people is the key purpose. Anonymity as a strategy for achieving honest responses is certainly a core assumption of the debaters. And I would agree that when someone asks for anonymous feedback, they encourage a certain mind-set in the rater that says, "I want you to be honest with me." (There are perhaps other ways besides anonymity to encourage such a mind-set, but that's a topic for another report.)

From my experience, accuracy of ratings and honesty of ratings are not necessarily the same thing. I can rate my husband low on punctuality, and that can be my honest assessment of him. But my perception might be driven by the few times that he was late, by my own impatience in waiting on other people, and by the generally higher standards I hold him to compared to standards I might hold for others. If I had been more "objective," realizing that the number of times he has been punctual far exceeds the times he has been late and using a more generally accepted standard of punctuality, then he might receive a higher rating. One rating may represent how I honestly feel, while the other represents a more accurate rating. The honest rating might be more important as a stimulus for a deeper understanding of our relationship; the objective rating might be more important if our neighborhood association were asking for an assessment of my husband as input in their selection of officers.

It is this accuracy mind-set that I think 360-degree assessment for administrative decision-making needs to work toward. Acknowledging that all ratings of other people will have an element of subjectivity, there are a number of strategies that could increase accuracy:

• Ratings are sought only from those people who have a close working relationship with the ratee.

• Raters rate only the dimensions they have ample opportunity to observe (peers and direct reports may rate different dimensions).

• Raters with the same relationship to the ratee (for instance, peers, direct reports, customers) work together to reach a consensus rating.

• Raters are educated to recognize their own rating biases.

• Raters are rewarded for providing assessment data that result in good decisions.

Just as the debaters took extreme positions to highlight the differences in their points of view, I have taken an extreme position that describes ideal contexts and processes needed to support either use of 360-degree assessments. The point of view that I am advocating is not that organizations should use 360-degree assessments only if they have the ideal conditions in place, but rather that they think through what they are trying to achieve with 360-degree assessments, what this means for how they should design the assessment process, what they can put in place to maximize the gain from these assessments, and how they will know if it's working. Taking an off-the-shelf instrument that was designed to provide in-depth feedback for development and adding it to an existing performance-appraisal process would be a sign to me that the organization hadn't thought these issues through. So would buying that same instrument in order to jump on the 360-degree-feedback bandwagon, using it for in-depth feedback but never embedding it in a larger development system that provides the opportunities, support, and rewards for growth and improvement. One of my biggest fears in either case is that people in the organization would conclude that the lack of success meant that 360-degree assessments were a bad idea and unknowingly throw away a powerful concept because it was poorly executed.

❧❧❧

Cynthia D. McCauley is a research scientist at the Center for Creative Leadership. She has been part of the research function since 1984 and has coauthored two of CCL's management-feedback instruments, *Benchmarks®* and the *Developmental Challenge Profile®: Learning from Job Experiences*. She has also conducted research on 360-degree feedback, the impact of leadership development programs, learning through job assignments, and developmental relationships. McCauley's most recent publication is "The Role of 360-degree Feedback in the Establishment of Learning Cultures" with

P. O. Wilson and L. Kelly-Radford in *Maximizing the Value of 360-degree Feedback: A Process for Successful Individual and Organizational Development* (Eds. W. Tornow, M. London, & CCL Associates; Jossey-Bass, March 1998). In addition, she has written several CCL reports and has published articles in a variety of journals, including *The Journal of Management, Journal of Applied Psychology,* and *Leadership Quarterly.* McCauley holds a Ph.D. in industrial/organizational psychology from the University of Georgia.

Ordering Information

To get more information, to order other CCL Press publications, or to find out about bulk-order discounts, please contact us by phone at 336-545-2810 or visit our online bookstore at **www.ccl.org/publications**.

CPSIA information can be obtained at www.ICGtesting.com
Printed in the USA
BVOW030453060212

282098BV00004B/6/A

9 781882 197316